CONSULTANT BOOK FOR ALL BUSINESS TYPE

Your step by step guide to success

By Onyema Uche Chigozie

Table of contents

STEPS TO MAINTAIN /MANAGE A
SUCCESSFUL BUSINESS

HOW TO SAVE A BUSINESS FROM
COLLAPSING

THINGS THAT HINDERS BUSINESS
PROGRESS

COMMON MISTAKES MADE BY
ENTERPRENEURS IN A BUSINESS

HOW TO PROMOTE YOUR BUSINESS

HOW TO WIN DEALS AND CONTRACTS IN YOUR BUSINESS

HOW TO ATTRACT CUSTOMERS TO YOUR BUSINESS

INTRODUCTION

Desiring to own, manage and be successful with your business with zero business idea, consultant book for all business type is your step by step guide to success. This book is written with experience and tested ideas. Business consulting book is a multipurpose business book packed with proven tactics, ground plan and perceptions to help you start, run and grow a lucrative and outstanding business with or without business ideas.

BUSINESS IN DETAILS

1.

Business is an economic system in which goods and services are exchanged in exchange for money. It is composed of individuals and organizations that are involved in the production, distribution, and exchange of goods and services.

Businesses can be categorized into four distinct types: manufacturing, retail, service, and information. Manufacturing businesses involve the production of goods while retail businesses involve the sale and distribution of goods. Service businesses involve providing customers with a service, such as a restaurant, while information businesses involve the gathering and exchange of information.

Businesses require capital to operate and require the utilization of resources such as land, labor, and capital. Business operations involve the use of marketing and advertising to reach potential customers, the use of accounting to ensure proper financial management, and the use of technology for efficient operation.

Businesses can be structured in different ways depending on the type of business. The most common types of business structures are sole proprietorships, partnerships, corporations, and limited liability companies. Each of these structures has advantages and disadvantages and should be carefully considered before the business is established.

The success of any business depends on the quality of its products and services, the effectiveness of its marketing plans, and the efficiency of its operations. A successful business must also have a clear, concise plan on how to achieve its goals and objectives.

In conclusion, business is an important economic system that involves the production, distribution, and exchange of goods and services. It requires capital, resources, and a clear plan in order to succeed.

2.

Business is an activity that involves the exchange of goods or services for money. It is a vital part of any economy, as it allows for the production, distribution and consumption of goods and services. Businesses can range from small, family-run operations to large multinational corporations.

Businesses are typically responsible for the production and distribution of goods or services. To do this, they must acquire, develop, and maintain resources such as raw materials, equipment, technology, and personnel. They also need to identify customers and markets and create strategies to market and sell their products. Businesses also need to manage finances and ensure they are profitable.

Businesses are usually formed by individuals, partnerships, or corporations. The legal structure of a business determines its responsibilities, liabilities, and rights. A business can be a sole proprietorship, partnership, limited liability company, or corporation. Depending on the structure, businesses must adhere to different rules and regulations.

Businesses have the potential to create wealth, provide employment, and contribute to the economic development of a country. However, they can also create risks, pollution, and other negative externalities. Therefore, businesses must be managed responsibly and ethically to ensure that their activities are beneficial to society.

Businesses can be divided into different sectors, such as services, retail, manufacturing, agriculture, and construction. Each sector has its own unique characteristics, such as the types of products and services offered, the processes used, the resources needed, and the regulations that must be followed.

Businesses need to be managed effectively to ensure their continued success. This includes strategic planning, financial management, product and service development, marketing, and customer service. Businesses require the right resources to succeed and must be able to adapt to changing market conditions.

In summary, business involves the exchange of goods and services for money. It is a vital part of any economy and requires the acquisition and development of resources, the identification of customers and markets, and the management of finances. Businesses come in different legal forms and can be divided into different sectors. Effective management is essential for businesses to succeed.

3.

Business is a process of creating, exchanging, and delivering products and services to customers. It involves activities that are done for the purpose of generating revenue and profits by creating customer satisfaction.

Businesses can be small, medium or large, and may operate for-profit or not-for-profit.

In business, there are many different activities that are necessary in order to be successful. These activities include marketing, product development, operations, finance, and human resources. Marketing involves creating and executing plans to reach potential customers. Product development involves creating products and services that meet customer needs and wants. Operations involve running the business and making sure that products and services are efficiently produced and delivered. Finance involves managing the financial resources of the business, such as budgeting, accounting, and taxation. Human resources involve recruiting, managing, and training employees.

Businesses also need to have an understanding of their industry and the competitive environment in which they operate. Companies must understand their customers, competitors, and the industry trends that can affect their business. They must also have a strategy for success and the resources to implement it.

Ultimately, businesses must have a plan for success and the ability to manage and execute it. This includes having a clear mission and vision, understanding the competitive environment and customer needs, and having the necessary resources to execute the plan. Businesses must also have the ability to adapt to changing customer and industry needs in order to remain competitive.

4.

Business is an economic activity that involves the exchange of goods, services, or both for remuneration. It is an essential component of the economy, providing organizations with an opportunity to generate revenue and generate value for the people they serve. Businesses come in all shapes and sizes, ranging from small, local operations to multinational corporations.

At its core, business is a way to create value and achieve success. It requires careful planning, sound decision-making, and efficient execution. Businesses must take into account their customers' needs and preferences, their competitors' strategies, and the ever-changing economic environment. To do this, businesses must have access to reliable information, resources, and technology.

Businesses can be divided into four main categories: production, marketing, finance, and operations. Production businesses create the goods and services that people use and consume. Marketing businesses are responsible for promoting and selling those goods and services. Financial businesses provide the capital necessary to facilitate the production and sale of goods and services. Operations businesses are responsible for the management of the production, marketing, and financial aspects of the business.

In addition to the four main categories, businesses must also consider the legal, ethical, and regulatory environment they operate in. Businesses must adhere to laws and regulations, understand their social and environmental impact, and strive to maintain relationships with customers, suppliers, and other stakeholders.

Finally, businesses must also consider their own internal processes, such as their operations, technology, and management structures. Businesses must ensure that they have the right people in place and the right processes in place to ensure that the business is operating efficiently and effectively.

In summary, business is an essential component of the economy. It requires careful planning, sound decision-making, and efficient execution. Businesses must understand their customers' needs and preferences, their competitors' strategies, and the ever-changing economic environment. They must also adhere to laws and regulations, understand their social and environmental impact, and strive to maintain relationships with customers, suppliers, and other stakeholders. Finally, businesses must have the right people and processes in place to ensure that the business is operating efficiently and effectively.

5.

Business is the activity of making one's living or making money by producing or buying and selling products (such as goods and services). It is a form of economic activity that is conducted within a certain legal and economic framework, and is defined by the laws of the land. It can also involve trading activities, such as manufacturing, warehousing, transportation, and marketing.

Businesses can be classified into four main categories: service, retail, manufacturing, and wholesale. Service businesses provide services to customers, such as legal, accounting, and consulting services. Retail businesses involve the sale of goods to consumers in small quantities. Manufacturing businesses produce goods that are then sold to either businesses or consumers. Wholesale businesses sell goods in bulk to other businesses.

A business can also be distinguished by its ownership structure. There are three main types of ownership structures: sole proprietorship, partnership, and corporation. In a sole proprietorship, the business is owned and operated by a single individual. In a partnership, two or more people share ownership and operate the business. In a corporation, ownership is shared among shareholders and the business is managed by a board of directors.

Businesses also have different types of operations. A business may be a for-profit entity, or it may be a nonprofit. For-profit businesses typically aim to maximize profits by providing goods and services to customers. Nonprofit organizations typically aim to provide a service to their customers at a lower cost or with a greater social benefit.

Finally, businesses can be characterized by their size. Small businesses are typically owned by an individual or a small group of people, while large businesses are typically owned by a large number of shareholders.

Overall, business is an important economic activity that involves creating and selling goods and services to customers. It is governed by laws and regulations, and can be owned and operated by individuals or companies of various sizes.

THINGS TO CONSIDER BEFORE STARTING A BUSINESS

1.

Starting a business is an exciting and rewarding endeavor, but it is important to consider a few basic things before you get started.

First, you need to determine what kind of business you want to create. Are you interested in launching a service-based business or a product-based business? Do you want to start a company from scratch or buy an existing business? Answering these questions will help you develop the framework for your new business.

Second, you need to do your research. Find out how much it will cost to start and run your business, and make sure you have enough capital to cover those costs. Also look into the legal requirements for starting and running a business in your area. You may need to apply for permits and licenses, as well as register your business with the government.

Third, you need to think about who your target customers are and develop a marketing plan. You need to figure out who will buy your product or service and how you will reach out to them. Research the competition and develop a plan for how you will stand out from them.

Fourth, you need to create a business plan. Your business plan should include details about how you plan to operate your business, a budget, and a timeline for achieving your goals. It should also include a risk assessment, so you can plan for potential issues that may arise.

Finally, you need to find a team to support you. You may need to hire employees, find an accountant, and partner with other businesses. You also need to decide if you need to outsource any services.

Starting a business is a lot of work, but if you take the time to consider these basic things before getting started, you will be better prepared to make your business a success.

2.

Starting a business is an exciting and rewarding journey, but it can also be a challenging one. Before taking the plunge, it's important to carefully consider some basic things.

First and foremost, you'll need to research and decide on a business idea. This should be something that you're passionate about, and that has potential to be successful. You'll need to research the market to assess the potential for profitability, as well as the financial investment that will be needed. Additionally, you'll need to think about the products or services you'll offer, and if there's an existing demand for them.

You'll also need to think about the legal and financial aspects of starting a business. You'll need to choose a business structure, such as a sole proprietorship or limited liability company, and register it with the state. You'll also need to consider any permits or licenses that may be required in your state. Additionally, you'll need to research local and federal tax laws to ensure that you're compliant.

In terms of funding, you'll need to consider how you'll finance your business. You may be able to get a business loan from a bank or other lender, or you may need to secure investors. Additionally, you'll need to think about the costs associated with running your business, such as rent, utilities, and payroll.

Finally, you'll need to consider the business's location. You may decide to work from home, or you may need to rent an office or retail space. You'll need to research the local market to determine the best location for your business. Additionally, if you'll be hiring employees, you'll need to consider their commute and the availability of parking.

Starting a business is a big undertaking, but with careful consideration and planning, it can be a rewarding and successful endeavor. By taking the time to research and plan ahead, you can set yourself up for success.

BUSINESS STEPS AND PROCEDURES

1.

Starting and running a successful business requires much more than simply having a great idea. It is important to establish a set of well-defined steps and procedures to ensure the business is able to operate efficiently and effectively.

The first step to setting up a business is to create a business plan. This document outlines the goals of the business, the strategies used to achieve them, the target market, and the resources needed to operate. It should also include a detailed financial plan and a risk management plan. The business plan should be reviewed and updated regularly to ensure that it is up to date and reflects current best practices.

The next step is to register the business with the relevant authorities. Depending on the type of business, this may involve filing paperwork with the local, state, and federal governments. For example, a sole proprietorship would need to register with the local government, while a corporation would need to register with the state and federal governments. It is important to make sure all the required paperwork is filed correctly to avoid any potential legal issues.

The next step is to secure the necessary funding for the business. This can be done through a variety of sources such as loans, investments, and grants. It is important to research the different options and determine which one is the best for the business.

The fourth step is to find and hire the right people for the business. This can involve researching the local job market, interviewing candidates, and conducting background checks. It is important to make sure the right people are hired for the right positions to ensure the business can operate effectively.

The fifth step is to create a marketing plan. This plan should outline the strategies used to reach potential customers, the budget allocated to marketing efforts, and the timeline for executing the plan. It is important to make sure the plan is regularly updated to reflect current trends and best practices.

Finally, it is important to create a system to track the progress of the business. This system should include goals, performance metrics, and any other relevant data. It is important to review this data regularly to ensure the business is on track and make any necessary adjustments.

These are the basic steps and procedures required to start and run a successful business. It is important to understand each of them and ensure they are followed correctly to ensure the business is able to operate efficiently and effectively.

2.
Business steps and procedures are important for any business to ensure that operations run smoothly and efficiently. It is essential to establish a well-defined set of steps and procedures for the business to follow. This helps to ensure that everyone involved in the business is on the same page when it comes to how tasks are completed and expectations are met.

The first step in establishing steps and procedures is to identify the key tasks that need to be completed. This involves analyzing the business's daily operations and determining which activities need to be completed in order to achieve the desired outcomes. Once the key tasks have been identified, it is important to create a step-by-step process for completing them. This process should be documented in a way that is clear and organized.

The next step is to assign specific roles and responsibilities to each member of the team. This ensures that everyone is aware of their duties and what is expected of them. This also helps to avoid potential conflicts and misunderstandings.

The third step is to develop a system for tracking progress and measuring success. This includes setting milestones and goals, as well as establishing metrics to measure how the business is performing. This helps to ensure that the business is on track and that its operations are running effectively.

The fourth step is to create a system for monitoring and evaluating performance. This involves reviewing the steps and procedures that have been established and making changes as needed. This helps to ensure that the business is improving and growing in the right direction.

Finally, it is important to review and update the steps and procedures on a regular basis. This helps to ensure that the business is taking the necessary steps to stay competitive and successful.

By following these steps and procedures, businesses can ensure that their operations are running smoothly and efficiently.

3.

Starting a business can be an exciting endeavor, but it is important to understand the business steps and procedures. This includes legal requirements, paperwork, and taxes, as well as how to create a business plan.

The first step is to determine the type of business entity you want to form. You can choose between a sole proprietorship, partnership, corporation, or limited liability company. Each of these has its own advantages and disadvantages, so it is important to research and understand the implications of each.

Once you have determined the business entity, you will need to register the business with the local, state, and federal governments. This will involve filing paperwork and paying appropriate taxes.

You may also need to obtain permits or licenses to legally operate your business.

The next step is to create a business plan. This plan should outline your business goals and objectives, as well as how you will achieve them. It should also include detailed information about your target market, your competitors, and your marketing strategies. Additionally, it should include financial statements, such as a budget and cash flow projections.

After the business plan is complete, you will need to secure financing. This may involve applying for loans or seeking investors. It is important to be aware of the interest rates and repayment terms associated with any loans you take out, as well as the risks associated with taking on investors.

Finally, you will need to obtain the necessary supplies and equipment needed to start the business. This includes office furniture, computers, and other materials. You may also need to hire staff to help with the day-to-day operations of the business.

Starting a business can be a daunting task, but with proper planning and research, it can be a rewarding experience. Understanding the business steps and procedures is essential to ensure that your business is successful.

STEPS TO MAINTAIN /MANAGE A SUCCESSFUL BUSINESS

1.

Managing a successful business requires a great deal of focus, attention, and hard work. To ensure success, it is important to develop and stick to a strategic plan that outlines a clear vision for the business, identifies the appropriate goals, and sets out a strategy for achieving them.

The first step to successful business management is to create a comprehensive business plan. This plan should include a mission statement that explains the purpose of the company and its objectives. It should also include an analysis of the external environment, such as the competitive landscape, legal and regulatory issues, and market trends. The business plan should also include an analysis of the internal environment, such as the company's strengths and weaknesses, resources, and capabilities. Additionally, the plan should include a competitive strategy that identifies the company's competitive advantages, strategies to increase market share, and a plan to respond to competitive pressures.

Once the business plan is in place, it is important to develop and implement strategies to achieve the goals set out in the plan. This involves developing strategies for marketing, production, finance, and operations. For example, a marketing strategy should include a plan to reach potential customers, create brand recognition, and generate leads. A production strategy should include a plan to develop, design, and produce products or services. A finance strategy should include a plan to manage the company's finances and ensure that it has sufficient resources to meet its objectives. And an operations strategy should include a plan to manage the company's day-to-day activities and ensure that its operations are efficient.

It is also important to create a culture that encourages collaboration, innovation, and risk-taking. This includes creating a culture of trust and respect between employees, allowing for open communication and feedback, and encouraging employees to come up with new ideas and solutions.

Finally, it is important to monitor and evaluate the progress of the business and make adjustments as needed. This includes monitoring customer feedback, sales figures, and financial performance. It also includes evaluating the effectiveness of the strategies that are being implemented and considering alternatives if necessary.

Overall, successful business management requires a great deal of focus, attention, and hard work. It is important to develop and implement a comprehensive business plan, create and implement strategies to achieve the goals set out in the plan, create a culture of collaboration, innovation, and risk-taking, and monitor and evaluate the progress of the business. By following these steps, businesses can ensure that they are well-positioned to succeed in the long run.

2.

Managing a successful business requires careful planning and dedication. The following steps can help you to create and maintain a successful business.

Step One: Create a Business Plan. A business plan is an important document that serves as a blueprint for your business. It outlines all the necessary information about your business, including your mission and vision, financial projections, and strategies for achieving success. It also provides an estimate of the resources needed to get the business off the ground and running.

Step Two: Secure Funding. Obtaining the necessary funding to start or grow a business can be a daunting task. It's important to research possible sources of funding and develop a plan for accessing that funding. Options include traditional loans from banks, venture capital, angel investments, crowdfunding and government grants.

Step Three: Research Your Market. It's essential to research your target market, including who your customers are, what they need and what they're willing to pay for it. Knowing your market will help you create products and services that are in demand and identify the best marketing channels to reach your target audience.

Step Four: Develop a Marketing Strategy. Developing an effective marketing strategy is key to the success of any business. Your marketing strategy should focus on how you'll reach your target audience, such as through advertising, public relations, content marketing, or social media.

Step Five: Build a Winning Team. Finding, recruiting and retaining top talent is essential for business success. It's important to build a team of employees who are committed to the success of your business and have the skills and experience needed to make it happen.

Step Six: Implement a Quality Control Process. Quality control is essential for any successful business. It's important to identify potential problems before they have a negative impact on your business and to develop a quality control process to ensure that your products and services meet customer expectations.

Step Seven: Monitor Your Progress. Businesses need to monitor their progress in order to identify areas for improvement and capitalize on strengths. Track your progress by regularly reviewing financial statements, customer feedback, and progress toward goals.

Step Eight: Adapt to Change. The business landscape is constantly changing, and successful businesses must be able to adapt to those changes. Pay attention to trends in your industry and customer needs, and be prepared to make changes to your business model as necessary.

By following these steps, you can create and maintain a successful business. It's important to remember that success doesn't happen overnight and requires dedication, hard work, and perseverance. With the right planning and effort, you can create a business that will thrive for years to come.

HOW TO SAVE A BUSINESS FROM COLLAPSING

Saving a business from collapsing is a challenging task that requires a strategic approach and a lot of hard work. Here are some steps that can be taken to save a business from collapsing:

Identify the problem: The first step in saving a business from collapsing is to identify the problem. It could be a lack of sales, poor cash flow, high expenses, or a combination of these factors. Conduct a thorough analysis of the business to identify the root cause of the problem.

Develop a plan: Once you have identified the problem, develop a plan to address it. The plan should include specific actions that need to be taken to address the problem. For example, if the problem is poor cash flow, the plan could include reducing expenses, increasing sales, or securing a loan.

Cut costs: One of the most effective ways to save a business from collapsing is to cut costs. Identify areas where costs can be reduced without impacting the quality of the product or service. This could include reducing staff, renegotiating contracts with suppliers, or moving to a cheaper location.

Increase sales: Increasing sales is another effective way to save a business from collapsing. Identify ways to attract new customers and retain existing ones. This could include launching a marketing campaign, offering discounts, or improving the quality of the product or service.

Secure additional funding: If the business is struggling to stay afloat, additional funding may be needed to keep it going. This could include securing a loan from a bank or other financial institution, seeking investment from a venture capitalist, or crowdfunding.

Seek professional help: If the problem is too complex to solve on your own, seek professional help. This could include hiring a consultant, accountant, or lawyer.

In summary, saving a business from collapsing requires a combination of strategic planning, cost-cutting, increasing sales, securing additional funding, and seeking professional help. It's important to act quickly and decisively to address the problem before it's too late

THINGS THAT HINDERS BUSINESS PROGRESS

There are several factors that can hinder business progress, including:

Lack of capital: One of the biggest obstacles to business progress is a lack of capital. Without sufficient funds, businesses may struggle to invest in new equipment, hire skilled employees, or expand into new markets.

Poor management: Another factor that can hinder business progress is poor management. This could include a lack of leadership, ineffective communication, or a failure to adapt to changing market conditions.

Competition: Competition can also hinder business progress, particularly if a business is operating in a crowded market. In order to succeed, businesses need to differentiate themselves from their competitors and offer unique value to customers.

Legal and regulatory issues: Legal and regulatory issues can also slow down business progress. For example, businesses may struggle to obtain necessary permits or licenses, or may face lawsuits or fines for non-compliance with regulations.

Technology: Rapidly changing technology can also hinder business progress, particularly if a business is slow to adopt new tools or platforms. Businesses need to stay up-to-date with the latest technology trends in order to remain competitive.

Economic conditions: Economic conditions can also impact business progress, particularly during times of recession or economic downturn. Businesses may struggle to attract customers or secure financing during these times, making it harder to grow and expand.

Inadequate infrastructure: Businesses that lack adequate infrastructure may also struggle to make progress. This may include outdated technology, inadequate facilities, or a lack of access to key resources. Without the right infrastructure in place, businesses may struggle to compete with more modern, well-equipped competitors.

Regulatory barriers: Regulatory barriers can also hinder business progress. This may include excessive licensing requirements, complex tax laws, or burdensome regulations that make it difficult for businesses to operate efficiently. These barriers can limit innovation, stifle competition, and make it difficult for businesses to grow and thrive.

Lack of innovation: Finally, a lack of innovation can also hinder business progress. Businesses that fail to innovate may struggle to keep up with changing customer needs and preferences, or may be outcompeted by more innovative rivals. Without a culture of innovation, businesses may struggle to stay relevant and competitive in today's fast-paced business environment.

In conclusion, there are several factors that can hinder business progress, including a lack of capital, poor management, inadequate infrastructure, regulatory barriers, economic conditions, and a lack of innovation. By addressing these challenges head-on, businesses can overcome these obstacles and achieve long-term success.

COMMON MISTAKES MADE BY ENTERPRENEURS IN A BUSINESS

Entrepreneurship is a challenging and rewarding journey, but it is not without its pitfalls. Many entrepreneurs make common mistakes that can hinder their progress and success. Here are some of the most common mistakes made by entrepreneurs:

Lack of planning: Many entrepreneurs jump into their business idea without a solid plan in place. This can lead to a lack of direction and focus, making it difficult to achieve long-term success.

Poor financial management: Entrepreneurs may also struggle with financial management, failing to keep track of their expenses or failing to secure sufficient funding to support the business. This can lead to cash flow problems and an inability to invest in growth opportunities.

Overestimating demand: Entrepreneurs may also make the mistake of overestimating demand for their product or service. This can lead to overproduction and excess inventory, which can be costly to store and manage.

Failure to adapt: In today's fast-paced business environment, entrepreneurs need to be able to adapt to changing market conditions. Failure to do so can result in missed opportunities and an inability to stay competitive.

Lack of focus: Entrepreneurs may also struggle with a lack of focus, trying to pursue too many opportunities at once. This can lead to a lack of progress and an inability to achieve business goals.

Poor hiring decisions: Finally, entrepreneurs may make poor hiring decisions, failing to hire the right people or failing to provide the necessary training and support to help employees succeed.

Lack of market research: One of the biggest mistakes entrepreneurs make is failing to conduct adequate market research. Without a clear understanding of their target market, competitors, and industry trends, entrepreneurs may struggle to develop a viable business plan and attract customers.

.

Underestimating costs: Entrepreneurs may also underestimate the costs of starting and running a business. This can lead to cash flow problems and a failure to invest in key areas of the business, such as marketing and infrastructure.

Failing to delegate: Many entrepreneurs are passionate about their business and want to be involved in every aspect of its operations. However, this can lead to burnout and a failure to delegate tasks to others. Entrepreneurs should focus on their strengths and delegate tasks to employees or contractors who can handle other aspects of the business.

Ignoring feedback: Entrepreneurs may also be resistant to feedback from customers, investors, or mentors. This can lead to a failure to adapt to changing market conditions or customer needs, and can hinder the growth of the business.

In summary, entrepreneurs can make a range of mistakes in their business, from a lack of planning and poor financial management to overestimating demand, failure to adapt, lack of focus, and poor hiring decisions. By being aware of these common mistakes and taking steps to avoid them, entrepreneurs can increase their chances of success and achieve their business goals.

HOW TO PROMOTE YOUR BUSINESS

1. Develop a Comprehensive Marketing Plan: A comprehensive marketing plan is essential for any business. It should include a detailed analysis of the target market, a description of the product or service, pricing strategies, promotional activities, and a timeline for implementation.

2. Utilize Social Media: Social media is a powerful tool for promoting a business. Create accounts on popular platforms

such as Facebook, Twitter, Instagram, and YouTube. Post regularly and engage with followers to build relationships and increase brand awareness.

3. Leverage Search Engine Optimization (SEO): SEO is a great way to increase visibility and drive traffic to your website. Optimize your website content with relevant keywords and phrases to improve your ranking in search engine results.

4. Create a Blog: A blog is a great way to share valuable content with your audience. Post regularly and include links to your website and social media accounts.

5. Network and Build Partnerships: Networking and building partnerships with other businesses can help you reach a larger audience. Consider hosting events, sponsoring local organizations, or partnering with influencers to promote your business.

6. Invest in Paid Advertising: Paid advertising can be an effective way to reach a larger audience. Consider investing in Google Ads

7. Define your target audience: Determine the demographics, interests, and behaviors of your ideal customers. This will help you tailor your promotions to attract and engage them.

8. Develop a marketing plan: Create a comprehensive marketing plan that includes different channels and tactics to reach your target audience. This can include social media marketing, email marketing, content marketing, search engine optimization, pay-per-click advertising, and more.

9. Build a strong brand: Establish a strong brand with a memorable name, logo, and tagline that reflects your business's values and personality. Make sure your branding...

In summary, Promoting a business is essential to attract customers, generate leads, build brand awareness, and ultimately increase sales.

HOW TO WIN DEALS AND CONTRACTS IN YOUR BUSINESS

Winning deals and contracts in business requires a combination of strategy, preparation, and execution.

1. Research the Client: Before you can win a deal or contract, you need to understand the client's needs and wants. Research the client's industry, competitors, and current market trends. This will help you craft a proposal that meets their needs and stands out from the competition.

2. Develop a Proposal: Once you have a good understanding of the client's needs, you can develop a proposal that meets their requirements. Make sure to include all the necessary information, such as pricing, timeline, and deliverables.

3. Present the Proposal: Presenting the proposal is the most important step in the process. Make sure to be prepared and confident when presenting. Be sure to answer any questions the client may have

and address any concerns they may have.

4. Negotiate: Once the proposal has been presented, it's time to negotiate. Be prepared to compromise and be flexible. Make sure to listen to the client's needs and be willing to make adjustments to the proposal if necessary.

5. Follow Up: Once the negotiation is complete, it is important to follow up with the other party to ensure that the deal and contract are finalized. This can be done

by sending a confirmation email or letter that outlines the details of the agreement. Additionally, it is important to ensure that all parties have signed the contract and that any payment terms have been met. Finally, it is important to keep track of the progress of the deal and contract to ensure that all parties are meeting their obligations.

HOW TO ATTRACT CUSTOMERS TO YOUR BUSINESS

I cannot provide a complete insight into your business. However, below are some general ways to attract customers to any business:

1. Know your target audience: Understanding your audience is crucial as it will enable you to tailor your services to meet their needs. Conduct market research and gather data that will help

you to understand what your target audience wants.

2. Develop a strong brand: Build a brand that is memorable and distinguishable from your competitors. Your brand should represent who you are and what you offer to your customers.

3. Establish a strong online presence: In today's digital age, customers expect businesses to have an online presence. Create a website, social media pages and

consider developing a blog to keep your customers updated.

4. Offer exceptional customer service: Your customers are the backbone of your business. You need to ensure that they are satisfied with your services. Train your employees to provide excellent customer service, respond promptly to inquiries and complaints, and go the extra mile to exceed customer expectations.

5. Develop marketing strategies: Marketing is essential if you want more

customers to find out about your business. Use a combination of online and offline marketing strategies such as advertising, email marketing, content marketing, and social media marketing to promote your business.

6. Offer promotions and discounts: Encourage customers to try your products or services by offering promotions and discounts. You can offer a discount on the first purchase, loyalty rewards, and referral bonuses.

7. Participate in community events: Engaging your business in community events such as charity drives, festivals, and volunteer work not only promotes your business but also helps you build strong relationships with your community. This helps your business gain more visibility and increases your brand reputation.

8. Monitor your online reputation: Your online reputation is a crucial aspect of your business's success. Stay on top of customer reviews on social media and

review sites, respond promptly to negative feedback, and showcase positive customer experiences on your social media pages and website.

9. Invest in technology: Technology is constantly evolving, and investing in it can help streamline your business operations and improve efficiency. Consider investing in customer relationship management (CRM) software to manage your customer data, project management software to optimize your team's workflow, and

marketing automation tools to streamline your marketing campaigns.

10. Attend industry events and conferences: Attending industry events and conferences not only helps you keep up with the latest trends and innovations in your field but also gives you the opportunity to network with other business owners and potential customers. Share your knowledge and learn from others, and you may even gain valuable business partnerships or collaborations.

Implementing these ten tips can help you grow and establish your business, but ultimately, the key to success is to always listen to your customers, provide excellent service or products, and adapt to the ever-changing market and consumer demands.